# POSITANO POCKET GUIDE

## Explore The Scenic Sidesea Paradise In Amalfi Coast, italy

**Orwell Travel's**

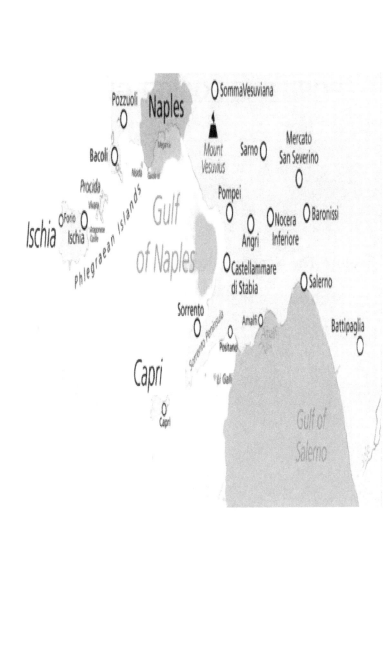

# CONTENTS

# INTRODUCTION

Positano is a stunning seaside town situated on the Amalfi Coast in southern Italy. Known for its stunning excellence, beguiling engineering, and beautiful scenes, Positano has turned into a famous vacationer location and a number one among craftsmen, journalists, and picture takers.

Settled on the bluffs of the Tyrrhenian Ocean, Positano flaunts dynamic pastel-shaded houses that fountain down the lofty slants, making a novel and extraordinary display. Its limited, winding roads are fixed with stores, craftsman shops, and comfortable bistros, adding to the town's heartfelt and charming air.

The historical backdrop of Positano traces all the way back to the Roman Domain when it filled in as a prosperous port. Throughout the long term, the town developed into a fishing town and in the end acquired distinction as a chic retreat objective during the twentieth hundred years. Today, it stays a well known place to get-away, drawing in guests from around the world who come to enjoy its excellence, loosen up on its unblemished sea shores, and investigate its rich social legacy.

Visitors to Positano can take part in a variety of activities and attractions. The Spiaggia Grande, the principal ocean side of the town, is a lively center where sightseers can absorb the Mediterranean sun and take a dunk in the completely clear waters. A more peaceful and private option is the Fornillo Beach, where you can relax and settle in peace.

Investigating the town by walking is a brilliant encounter, permitting guests to find unlikely treasures like the Congregation of St Nick Maria Assunta with its striking vault and the middle age Torre Trasita, a lookout that offers all encompassing perspectives on the shore. The Way of the Divine beings (Sentiero degli Dei) is a famous climbing trail that gives stunning vistas of the encompassing bluffs, ocean, and adjoining towns.

Culinary devotees will get a kick out of the nearby food, which includes new fish, dynamic flavors, and customary dishes. Additionally, Positano is well-known for its renowned Limoncello liqueur, which is made from the abundance of lemons in the area.

Positano is a destination that captivates and leaves an indelible impression on its visitors, whether you're looking for relaxation, natural beauty, cultural exploration, or just a romantic getaway. It is a dreamlike getaway on the stunning Amalfi Coast in Italy due to its timeless appeal and idyllic setting.

# CHAPTER ONE

## POSITANO

Positano is a lovely beach front town situated on the Amalfi Coast in southern Italy. Some responses to your inquiries are as follows:

### When to go

The late spring and early autumn (September to October) are the best times to visit Positano. During these months, the weather conditions is lovely, and the vacationer swarms are somewhat more modest contrasted with the pinnacle summer season. However, you can also visit in July and August if you like warmer weather and don't mind more people.

### How to get there?

The closest global air terminal to Positano is Naples international airport. From the air terminal, you can take an immediate transport or taxi to Positano, which is roughly a 1.5 to 2-hour drive away. On the other hand, you can likewise take a train from Naples to Sorrento and afterward get a ship or transport to Positano.

### What to pack?

While visiting Positano, it's really smart to pack lightweight and happy with dress appropriate for warm Mediterranean climate. The following are essential items:

Clothing like shorts, t-shirts, sundresses, and skirts that is lightweight and breathable.

Swimwear, as Positano has delightful sea shores.

Comfortable shoes for walking, as the village has narrow, steep streets.

For sun protection, wear sunglasses, a hat, and sunscreen.

a light jacket or sweater for the cooler evenings, particularly if you visit in the spring or fall.

## Currency exchange, visas, and vaccinations

Currency: The Euro (€) is Italy's official currency. You can trade cash at banks, trade workplaces, or use ATMs in Positano. Mastercards are broadly acknowledged in many spots.

Visas: Depending on your nationality, you may or may not require a visa to visit Italy. With a valid passport or national ID card, you can enter Italy if you are a citizen of the European Union or Schengen Area. Visitors from numerous other nations, including the United States, Canada, Australia, and New Zealand, do not need a visa to enter Italy for up to 90 days. However, you should check with the Italian embassy or consulate in your country for the most up-to-date information because visa requirements may vary.

Vaccinations: There are no particular immunizations expected for heading out to Positano or Italy overall. However, keeping up with routine vaccinations is always a good idea. In addition, it's a good idea to check with your doctor or a travel clinic well in advance of your trip to see if any particular vaccinations or health precautions are needed.

It is essential to keep in mind that health recommendations, visa requirements, and travel restrictions can change over time. Therefore, in order to ensure that you have the most up-to-date and accurate information, it is always a good idea to consult official sources, such as the Italian embassy or consulate, prior to your trip.

# CHAPTER TWO

## GETTING AROUND

Within and around Positano, there are a few different options for transportation.

### Bus service

The SITA transport is the least expensive method for getting around Positano. It stops at all of the major landmarks and runs along the main road, Viale Pasitea. A single ticket costs €1.50, while a day pass costs €2.50.

### Taxi

Taxis are a more expensive option, but if you are traveling with a group or have a lot of luggage, they may be more convenient. Taxis can be booked in advance or rented out on the street.

### E-scooter

Positano can be explored in a fun and eco-friendly way with e-scooters. They are available for rent from a variety of local businesses. A typical hourly rate of around €15 or €50 per day is charged.

## Walking

Positano is a somewhat unassuming community and can be handily investigated by walking. Take your time and enjoy the walk because the views from the streets and stairways are breathtaking.

On the off chance that you are going to Positano from different urban communities in Italy, there are a few train and ship choices accessible.

## Train

From other cities in Italy, the most common way to get to Positano is by train. Positano is reached by train from Naples, Salerno, and Sorrento. From Naples, the trip takes about two hours and thirty minutes, from Salerno, about one hour and thirty minutes, and from Sorrento, about thirty minutes.

You can use the most popular train station in Positano which is Porto di Positano

## Ferry

Positano can be reached from other Amalfi Coast cities via scenic ferry. Ships run from Naples, Salerno, Amalfi, and Capri to Positano. The journey takes approximately one hour and thirty minutes from Naples, approximately thirty minutes from Salerno, approximately fifteen minutes from Amalfi, and approximately forty-five minutes from Capri.

Regardless of how you decide to get around Positano, you make certain to partake in your time in this gorgeous town.

## Neighboring towns near Positano

Here are a portion of the neighboring towns close to Positano

### Praiano

Positano is just three kilometers (two miles) away in the small town of Praiano. It is known for its wonderful sea shores, cliffside area, and vivid houses. You can get to Praiano by bus, car, or boat.

### Ravello

It is a town about 5 kilometers (three miles) above Positano. It is well-known for its world-famous gardens, luxurious hotels, and stunning views. You can get to Ravello by bus, car, or taxi.

### Amalfi

Amalfi is the largest town on the Amalfi Coast. It is known for its noteworthy focus, Duomo, and beautiful houses. You can get to Amalfi by bus, car, or boat.

### Minori

It is a small town about 4 km (2.5 mi) away from Amalfi. It is well-known for its lemon groves, historic district, and beaches. You can get to Minori by bus, car, or boat.

## Scala

It is a small town about 3 km (2 mi) from Amalfi. [Image of Minori, a town near Positano] It is known for its wonderful perspectives, climbing trails, and Limoncello creation. You can get to Scala by bus, car, or taxi.

### Here are a portion of what to see and do in these neighboring towns

Visit the notable centers of these towns, which are brimming with restricted roads, brilliantly shaded houses, and exceptionally old chapels.

Visit the beaches in these towns, which are known for their clear waters, soft sand, and stunning views.

Go hiking in the slopes or mountains behind these towns, where you can appreciate dazzling perspectives on the coast.

Take a boat trip along the Amalfi Coast to see the towns from the water and swim in the clear waters.

Taste the local cuisine, which includes pasta, limoncello, and fresh seafood.

**Go to a music or cultural event in one of these towns, which frequently host concerts, festivals, and other events.**

# CHAPTER THREE

## BEACHES AND ISLANDS

## Spiaggia Grande

### History

The historical backdrop of Spiaggia Grande in Positano traces all the way back to antiquated times. The earliest evidence of a settlement in the area dates back to the Paleolithic period, and the beach has long been a popular vacation spot for both locals and tourists.

Spiaggia Grande was a popular vacation spot for wealthy Romans during the Roman era. The remnants of a Roman estate have been tracked down close to the ocean side, and it is accepted that the manor was utilized by Roman sovereigns and different individuals from the tip top.

Positano was a thriving port town in the Middle Ages. The town's area on the Amalfi Coast made it a significant exchanging focus, and Spiaggia Grande was a significant center for transportation and trade.

In the sixteenth and seventeenth hundreds of years, Positano was perhaps of the richest town in the area. The town's economy depended on exchange, fishing, and shipbuilding, and Spiaggia Grande was a significant community for these exercises.

In the nineteenth hundred years, Positano started to draw in sightseers from everywhere the world. Artists, writers, and other creative individuals made the town a popular destination due to its stunning views, charming architecture, and stunning beaches.

Today, Spiaggia Grande is one of the most famous traveler objections in Italy. The ocean side is known for its reasonable blue waters, delicate sand, and dazzling perspectives on the Amalfi Coast. Spiaggia Grande is likewise home to various eateries, bars, and shops, making it an incredible spot to go through a day unwinding and partaking in the Italian Riviera.

Additional historical information about Spiaggia Grande includes the

<u>following</u>

Originally, the beach was called "Spiaggia dei Conigli" (Rabbit Beach) due to the large number of rabbits that lived there.

In the 19th century, the beach was renamed "Spiaggia Grande" (Big Beach) to reflect its size and popularity.

The ocean side was utilized as an arrival site for Partnered powers during The Second Great War.

The beach was featured in the 1951 movie "A Place in the Sun," which starred Montgomery Clift and Elizabeth Taylor.

The ocean side has been positioned as quite possibly of the most lovely ocean side on the planet by various travel distributions.

The main beach in Positano, Italy's Campania region, is Spiaggia Grande. It is a long, sandy ocean side with clear blue waters and staggering perspectives on the Amalfi Coast. The ocean side is separated into two segments: the public region and the ocean side clubs. Although access to the public area is free, especially during the summer, it can get crowded. The ocean side clubs offer a more sumptuous encounter, with sunbeds, umbrellas, and server administration.

<u>Here are the ways of getting to Spiaggia Grande</u>

Walking: The ocean side is situated in the focal point of Positano, so it is effectively open by walking. Take the steps down to the beach from Piazza dei Mulini, the main square.

By transport: Spiaggia Grande is close to a number of bus stops. From Salerno and Amalfi, the SITA bus line goes to Positano.

By car: There is a little parking garage close to Spiaggia Grande, yet it tops off rapidly in the late spring months. If you are driving, the best way to get to the beach is to park in one of Positano's larger parking lots and walk there.

The prices you pay for Spiaggia Grande depend on which part of the beach you choose. Access to the public area is free, but sunbeds and umbrellas from the beach clubs cost money. The typical daily charges range from €15 to €20.

The services at Spiaggia Grande vary depending on where you choose to stay on the beach. There are a few small bars and restaurants in the public area, but the beach clubs have more services like wait staff, changing rooms, and showers.

Spiaggia Grande is open from 9am to 7pm, however the ocean side clubs might have prior or later opening times.

There are various fun exercises you can appreciate at Spiaggia Grande, like swimming, sunbathing, swimming, and plunging. There are likewise various boat visits and journeys that leave from the ocean side.

It is recommended that you wear water shoes if you intend to swim at Spiaggia Grande because the rocks can be slick. Because the sun can be very strong during the summer, you might also want to bring a hat and sunscreen with you.

There are various cafés and bars situated close to Spiaggia Grande, so you can without much of a stretch track down something to eat or drink. Probably the most famous cafés include

Il Cavatappi: This café serves conventional Italian pasta dishes and fish.

La Sponda: The rooftop terrace of this restaurant offers breathtaking views of the Amalfi Coast.

Lo Scoglio: Fresh seafood dishes are available at this beachfront restaurant.

There are also a few small bars and cafes near the beach where you can get drinks and food.

## Fornillo Beach

Fornillo Ocean side is a little, separated ocean side situated in Positano, Italy. It is known for its completely clear waters, delicate sand, and loosened up air. The ocean side is encircled by bluffs and pine trees, which give shade and security.

## History

The history of Fornillo Beach goes back to the 15th century. The ocean side was initially utilized by anglers and ranchers, however it in the end turned into a well known traveler objective. A number of private beach clubs were built on the beach at the beginning of the 1900s, and ever since, it has been a popular spot for swimming and sunbathing.

## How to get there

Fornillo Beach is about 1.2 miles (2.5 kilometers) from Positano's center. From the town center, you can get there by walking down the steps. There is likewise a transport that stops close to the ocean side.

Access to the public beach at Fornillo is free.

## Fees

Sunbeds and umbrellas, on the other hand, are available for a fee at a number of private beach clubs.

## Service

The public ocean side at Fornillo has various conveniences, including showers, latrines, and a lifeguard station. There are likewise various eateries and bars situated close to the ocean side.

The public beach at Fornillo is open daily from 9 a.m. to 7 p.m. The confidential ocean side clubs might have various active times.

## Fun exercises there

Fornillo Ocean side is an incredible spot to unwind and partake in the sun and sand. There are likewise various fun exercises that you can appreciate, like swimming, sunbathing, swimming, and plunging.

## Outfit to go with

The best outfit to wear to Fornillo Ocean side is something agreeable and cool. A swimsuit, coverup, hat, and sunglasses are all essentials. You might also want to bring a towel, a bottle of water, and sunscreen.

## restaurants

There are a lot of bars and restaurants near Fornillo Beach. Fresh seafood, pasta, pizza, and cocktails are just a few of the dishes and drinks available at these establishments.

The following are some of the bars and restaurants near Fornillo Beach:

Lido La Scogliera is a famous ocean side club that offers sunbeds, umbrellas, and a café with all encompassing perspectives on the ocean.

Bar Il Pirata is a little bar found right near the ocean that serves beverages and bites.

Ristorante Il Cavatappi is an Italian restaurant in Positano that serves a variety of dishes.

Ristorante Positano Mare** is another Positano-area restaurant that serves a variety of Italian dishes with a view of the sea.

## Arienzo Beach

Arienzo Beach is a tiny bay in Positano, Italy, on the Amalfi Coast. It is a beach that is half public and half private. The public section can be reached via a long staircase, while the private section can be reached via a private shuttle. The beach is well-known for its crystal-clear water, white sand, and breathtaking views of the cliffs that surround it.

### History

Arienzo Ocean side has been a well known traveler objective since the mid 1900s. It was a remote beach that could only be reached by boat in the past. But in the 1950s, a staircase was built to get to the beach, making it easier for tourists to get there. During the 1970s, the principal ocean side club opened on Arienzo Ocean side, and it has since become one of the most well known ocean side clubs on the Amalfi Coast.

### How to get there

A long staircase that begins on the main road in Positano leads to the public section of Arienzo Beach. The confidential part of the ocean side can be arrived at by confidential transport, what withdraws from the principal street in Positano.

### Fees

Access to the public section of Arienzo Beach is free. The confidential part of the ocean side charges an expense for sunbeds and umbrellas. The expense additionally incorporates admittance to the ocean side club's offices, like the bar, eatery, and pool.

## Service

The ocean side club at Arienzo Ocean side offers different administrations, including sunbeds and umbrellas, a bar, a café, and a pool. Italian cuisine and beverages are available at the restaurant and bar. From May to September or first week of October, you can use the pool.

## Time of opening and closing

The public area of Arienzo Beach is open from 9 a.m. to 7 p.m. The confidential segment of the ocean side is open from 8am to 7pm.

## Fun exercises there

There are various fun exercises that can be appreciated at Arienzo Ocean side, like swimming, sunbathing, swimming, and kayaking. A small area for cliff jumping is also close to the private beach.

## Outfit to go with

Swimming and sunbathing at Arienzo Beach require a swimsuit. To shield yourself from the sun, you might also want to bring sunglasses, a hoodie, and a coverup. You will also need to bring the appropriate clothing and equipment if you intend to participate in any water-based activities like kayaking or snorkeling.

The beach club at Arienzo Beach has a restaurant that serves a variety of Italian cuisine. Eating options are also available. Positano also has a few restaurants and cafes that are just a short walk from the beach.

Here are a few restaurants close to Arienzo Ocean side

The Cavatappi This eatery serves conventional Italian dishes in a comfortable setting.

La Sponda: This eatery has a lovely perspective on the ocean and serves new fish dishes.

 Lo Scoglio: This café is known for its pizzas and pasta dishes.

## Laurito Beach

Laurito Ocean side is a little, detached ocean side situated in Positano, Italy. It is well-known for its crystal-clear waters, white sand, and views of the cliffs. Swimming, sunbathing, and cliff jumping are all popular activities at the beach.

History

Laurito Ocean side was initially a confidential ocean side claimed by the Bella family. In 1966, Adolfo Bella opened an eatery on the ocean front called Da Adolfo. Locals and tourists alike quickly became regulars at the restaurant. The Bella family established a public beach area adjacent to the restaurant in 1980.

## How to get there

Laurito Ocean side is situated around a 20-minute stroll from the focal point of Positano. You can likewise take a taxi or the transport to the ocean side.

There are no fees to use the Laurito Beach public beach area. Sunbeds and umbrellas, on the other hand, are subject to a fee. The café at Da Adolfo likewise has an expense for food and beverages.

## Service

A lifeguard is on duty at the public beach area of Laurito Beach. There are likewise a couple of little shops and eateries situated close to the ocean side.

## opening and closing

From May to October, the public beach area at Laurito Beach is open. The active times differ contingent upon the season.

### Fun exercises there

As well as swimming, sunbathing, and precipice bouncing, there are a couple of other fun exercises that you can appreciate at Laurito Ocean side. These include:

Swimming and making a plunge the reasonable waters off the shore of the ocean side

Climbing or trekking to the ocean side along the cliffside trails

Going on a boat outing to investigate the close by islands

### Outfit to go with

The best outfit to wear to Laurito Ocean side is something agreeable and light. You will need to wear a bathing suit, conceal, and shades. Additionally, you might want to bring a hat and sunblock.

### There are a few restaurants close to Laurito Beach.

Da Adolfo, which is right on the beach, is the most popular restaurant. Da Adolfo serves pizza, pasta, grilled seafood, and other traditional Italian dishes. There are likewise a couple of little bistros and bars situated close to the ocean side.

## ISLANDS CLOSE TO POSITANO

### Island of Ischia

The top island outside Positano is Ischia. It is the biggest island in the Bay of Naples and is known for its warm waters, sea shores, and climbing trails. Ischia can be reached by ferry or hydrofoil, and it is about 40 kilometers from Positano.

## Other islands near Positano include the following

### Procida

This island is known for its beautiful houses and its notable place. By ferry or hydrofoil, Procida, which is about 30 kilometers from Positano, can be reached.

### Capri

The Faraglioni cliffs, the Blue Grotto, and the glamorous resorts on this island are all well-known. Capri is situated around 20 kilometers from

Positano and can be reached by ship or hydrofoil.

## Islands of Li Galli

These three islets are found simply inverse Positano and are known for their excellence and their set of experiences. The Li Galli Islands are exclusive and are not open to general society.

Eventually, the best island to visit close Positano relies upon your inclinations. Ischia is a great destination for a relaxing vacation with numerous thermal water options. Capri might be a better choice if you're looking for a lively and glamorous atmosphere. Additionally, the Li Galli Islands may be the ideal location for a private and secluded island escape.

# CHAPTER FOUR

## POSITANO TOUR FOR KIDS

Here are a pleasant activities in Positano with kids

Visit the Fornillo beach.

Children will enjoy swimming and playing in the sand at this small beach because it is protected from the wind and waves.

Visit the MAR - Museo Archeologico Romano Positano.

Roman artifacts from the area can be found in this small museum. The antique jewelry, pottery, and statues will appeal to children.

Eat at the Arienzo Ocean side Club.

The playground and kids' menu at this beach club let kids run around and play while parents relax and take in the view.

Visit the Chiesa di St Nick Maria Assunta e Cripta Medievale.

The oldest church in Positano has a beautiful crypt. Kids will have a great time exploring the underground rooms.

"Spend the day at Spiaggia Grande.This enormous ocean side is the most well known in Positano and has a lot of room for youngsters to go around and play.


Go on a boat outing to the Emerald Grotto.

The stunning emerald-colored waters of this cave are famous. Children will cherish investigating the cavern and swimming in the perfectly clear water.

Go hiking in the hills above Positano.

There are numerous hiking trails that lead to breathtaking vistas of the town and coastline. Children will partake in the test of climbing and the feeling of achievement at the top.


Here are a few extra ways to visit Positano with kids

Wear agreeable shoes, as there will be a ton of strolling involved.

 Bring a carriage or transporter for small kids, as a portion of the ways can be steep and thin.

Bring plenty of water and sunblock because Positano can get hot, especially in the summer.

Know about the tides, as certain sea shores can be risky at elevated tide.

Rest and refuel throughout the day by taking breaks.

Above all else, have fun! With kids, Positano is a beautiful place to visit.


## Shopping and top markets in Positano

Positano is a great place to shop, particularly for luxury and fashion items. Along the main streets of the town, like Via Cristoforo Colombo and Via dei Mulini, there are a lot of designer shops and high-end boutiques.

## Here are a portion of the top markets in Positano

### Positano street Market

Every Wednesday morning, this market is open from 8 a.m. to 1 p.m. It's situated in the town place, close to the port. You can track down new produce, keepsakes, and different products at this market.

### Maiori Street Market

This market happens each Friday morning from 8am to 1pm. It's situated in the town of Maiori, which is around a 15-minute drive from Positano. You can track down new produce, trinkets, and different products at this market.

### Praiano street Market

This market happens each Sunday morning from 8am to 1pm. It is in the town of Praiano, about 20 minutes from Positano by car. You can track down new produce, keepsakes, and different merchandise at this market.

To get to the Positano Road Market, you can walk or take the transport. The bus station is situated close to the port. To get to the Maiori and

Praiano street Markets, you can drive or take the transport. The bus station is situated in the town focus of every town.

## Here are a few tips when shopping in Positano

 Be ready to spend cash. Prices are higher in Positano than in other parts of Italy because it is a destination for luxury.

The markets are a great place to look for mementos to take home. At the markets, you can also find unique items like jewelry and ceramics made by hand.

 In the event that you're on a tight spending plan, there are still a few extraordinary spots to shop in Positano. A number of smaller boutiques and shops that sell clothing, accessories, and souvenirs at prices that are more reasonable can be found on side streets away from the main piazza.

 Make certain to deal. It's not unexpected to deal in Italy, so feel free to request a lower cost, particularly at the business sectors.

Partake in the experience. Positano shopping is a great way to learn about the local culture and atmosphere. Enjoy the sunshine, observe the locals, and shop.

# CHAPTER FIVE

## TOP MUSEUMS AND ART GALLERIES

### The Museo Archeologico Romano di Positano

it is an archeological exhibition hall in Positano, Italy. It houses a collection of Roman villa finds that were found under the Church of Santa Maria Assunta in the early 1900s. The villa was constructed in the first century AD and was demolished in 79 AD when Mount Vesuvius erupted. The exhibition hall's assortment incorporates frescoes, mosaics, figures, and different antiques from the manor.

#### History

The disclosure of the Roman estate in Positano traces all the way back to the mid 1900s. In 1920, a butcher was digging a channel in the yard of the Congregation of St Nick Maria Assunta when he went over a progression of underground loads. These chambers were subsequently exhumed and found to contain the remaining parts of a huge Roman manor. The manor was implicit the first century Promotion and was obliterated by the ejection of Mount Vesuvius in 79 Advertisement.

For several decades, the Roman villa in Positano was excavated. The Italian government made the decision to construct a museum to house the villa's finds in the 1960s. The historical center opened in 1976 and was named the Museo Archeologico Romano di Positano (Blemish).

## How to get there

The Museo Archeologico Romano di Positano is situated in the core of Positano, close to the Congregation of St Nick Maria Assunta. The museum is easily reached by car or on foot. There is a parking lot close to the museum if you are driving there.

## Fees

The extra charge to the Museo Archeologico Romano di Positano is €6 for grown-ups and €4 for youngsters. There is likewise a diminished charge for understudies and seniors.

## Service

The Museo Archeologico Romano di Positano is open from 9:00 am to 7:00 pm, seven days every week. The historical center is shut on January 1, May 1, and December 25.

## Opening/shutting time

The Museo Archeologico Romano di Positano is open from 9:00 am to 7:00 pm, seven days per week. On January 1, May 1, and December 25, the museum is closed.

## Fun things to do there

Visitors to the Museo Archeologico Romano di Positano can do more than just look at the exhibits. They can also participate in a variety of other activities. Among these are the following:

Taking a directed visit through the exhibition hall

Going to an exceptional occasion or show

Loosening up in the exhibition hall's nursery

Partaking in a feast at one of the numerous eateries close by

## Restaurants in or nearby

There are numerous restaurants situated in or close to the Museo Archeologico Romano di Positano. The following are some of the most well-liked eateries

Il Cavatappi

Il Fiordo

Lo Scoglio

La Sponda

These restaurants offer an assortment of Italian cooking, with some spend significant time in fish dishes. All of them are within a short walk of the museum, making them an easy choice for lunch or dinner after a museum visit.

## Miniaci Art Gallery

In the center of Positano, Italy, is the independent, small Miniaci Art

Gallery. It was established in 1990 by craftsman and gallerist Michele Miniaci, who has been gathering and showing contemporary workmanship from around the world for more than 30 years. The paintings, sculptures, photographs, and mixed-media works in the gallery's collection span a broad spectrum of media. Specialists addressed at the display incorporate both laid out and arising names, and the display has normal presentations and occasions.

## History

 The Miniaci Art Gallery was established in 1990 by Positano-born Michele Miniaci. In order to share his enthusiasm for contemporary art with the world, Miniaci opened the gallery in the 1970s. The first show at the gallery featured works by local artists, but Miniaci soon started showing work by artists from all over the world. Over 500 pieces of art are in the gallery's collection today, and it holds regular events and exhibitions.

## How to get there

The Miniaci Art Gallery is on the main street (Via dei Mulini) in the heart of Positano. It is a short stroll from the ocean side and the Duomo. The town square (Piazza dei Mulini) has the closest public parking.

## Fees

The Miniaci Art Gallery does not charge admission. In any case, gifts are gladly received.

## Service

 The gallery is open seven days a week from 10:00 AM to 7:00 PM. The staff is warm and knowledgeable, and they are happy to discuss the art with you.

The Miniaci Art Gallery is open seven days a week, from 10:00 a.m. to 7:00 p.m.

## Fun exercises there

As well as review the craftsmanship, guests can likewise partake in various different exercises at the Miniaci Workmanship Display. The display has customary shows and occasions, and it likewise offers workmanship classes and studios. Guests can likewise partake in the wonderful perspectives on Positano from the exhibition's patio.

## Restaurants within or near the Miniaci Art Gallery

There are numerous restaurants within or near the gallery. The following are some of the most well-liked eateries:

The Cavatappi In a charming setting, this restaurant serves traditional Italian cuisine.

La Sponda: This café has a delightful patio with staggering perspectives on the Amalfi Coast.

 Lo Scoglio: This eatery is known for its new fish dishes.

 Il Pirata: This lively restaurant is a popular destination for both locals and tourists alike.

## Absolute Positano

Outright Positano is an exhibition and shop selling canvases, Murano glass, earthenware production, and different trinkets in Positano, Italy. Piazza dei Mulini, a picturesque square in the center of the town, is where it is situated.

Irene De Michele, a local artist and entrepreneur, established the gallery in 1995. She first started selling her own paintings, but she soon started selling those of other local artists and craftspeople as well. Today, Outright Positano has a wide determination of excellent handcrafted Italian items.

The exhibition is open lasting through the year, from 9am to 7pm. There is no admission fee, but if you find something you like, you are encouraged to buy it. Friendly and helpful, the staff is happy to answer any questions you may have.

At Absolute Positano, you can engage in a wide range of activities in addition to shopping. On the premises, there is a small cafe where you can unwind with a beverage or snack. You can likewise take a composition class or studio, or essentially peruse the display and respect the lovely work of art.

Absolute Positano is the ideal location to shop if you're looking for a one-of-a-kind keepsake of your trip to Positano. From a stunning painting to a piece of Murano glass, you are sure to find something you love.

<u>Some eateries can be found within or near Absolute Positano</u>

Il Cavatappi: This eatery is found right close to Outright Positano. It serves seafood-focused traditional Italian cuisine.

La Sponda: This restaurant is on a cliff with a view of the sea. It has beautiful views and good food.

Il Fiordo: This eatery is situated in a collapse the cliffside. It has a heartfelt air and serves inventive Italian food.

Lo Scoglio: This eatery is situated on a little ocean side. Fresh seafood and views of the Amalfi Coast are at their best here.

To get to Outright Positano, you can take the train to Positano station. The gallery can be reached in a short walk from the station. Positano can also be reached by bus. Near the gallery is the bus stop.

## Other top sites in Positano

Famous sites can be found in Positano

<u>The path of the Gods (Sentiero degli Dei)</u>

It is a difficult 5-mile climb with staggering perspectives on the Amalfi Coast.

### The Chiesa di St Nick Maria Assunta e Cripta Medievale

It is the fundamental church in Positano, with a wonderful ringer tower and a sepulcher tracing all the way back to the twelfth 100 years.

### Grotta dello Smeraldo

A sea cave with waters that are an emerald green is known as the "Grotta dello Smeraldo." It tends to be reached by boat or by a short climb.

### Tennis Al Settimo Piano in Positano

The tennis club known as "Tennis Al Settimo Piano" can be found on the seventh floor of a cliffside building. The Amalfi Coast is clearly visible from this location.

### The Positano Fashion

It is known for its splendidly shaded clothing and adornments.

These are only a couple of the numerous renowned things to see in Positano. Positano is a must-visit destination for any traveler due to its stunning scenery, charming shops, and delectable cuisine.

# CHAPTER SIX

## ACCOMMODATION

The following are some of Positano's best and cheapest hotels

### Best hotels

The luxury hotel Le Sirenuse is one of the "Best Hotels in Positano." It has stunning views of the Amalfi Coast. It has a Michelin-featured eatery, a confidential ocean side, and a housetop pool.

Il San Pietro di Positano is another luxurious hotel with stunning views and a location on a cliffside. It has a spa, a tennis court, and a pool.

Palazzo Murat is a noteworthy inn with rich rooms and a focal area. It has a rooftop terrace with sea and town views.

Hotel Marincanto is a boutique hotel with stunning sea views and a private location. It has a swimming pool and a private beach.

The Hotel Poseidon is a budget-friendly hotel with a central location and sea views. It has a roof patio and a bar.

## Cheapest hotels in Positano

Ostello Brikette is an inn with an assortment of apartments and confidential rooms. A common area and kitchen are shared in it.

Residence La Dolce Vita  is a Positano apartment rental with fully equipped apartments. With views of the town and the sea, it is in the upper part of Positano.

Florida Residence is a place to rent fully furnished apartments. It is close to the beach and in the lower part of Positano.

La Caravella di Positano, Residence is a loft rental with completely prepared condos. With views of the town and the sea, it is in the upper part of Positano.

Casa Teresa is a bed and breakfast that has a variety of rooms, some of which have views of the sea. It is close to the beach and in the lower part of Positano.

These are just a few of the many hotels in Positano. Before making a reservation for your stay, it's critical to conduct research and compare prices.

Note : The price to spend the night at this hotels are not stated due to continuous increase or decrease in their lodging price

This list are classified into two categories to help you know where to start looking for in a case you have a low or high buget.

# CHAPTER SEVEN

## HISTORICAL PLACES IN POSITANO

Here are a portion of the historical spots in Positano and how to visit them

The most important church in Positano is the Chiiesa di Santa Maria Assunta e Cripta Medievale. It is situated in the focal point of town and can be effortlessly arrived at by walking. There is no extra charge, however gifts are valued. Every day, the church is open from 9 a.m. to 6 p.m. A Byzantine icon of the Virgin Mary from the 13th century can be seen inside the church, along with other religious artworks. There is likewise a grave under the congregation that traces all the way back to the eleventh hundred years.

Sentiero degli Dei is a climbing trail that runs along the bluffs above Positano. It offers dazzling perspectives on the shoreline and is a well known method for understanding the town according to with an improved point of view. The 5.8-kilometer trail can be completed in about three hours. There are a few spots to begin the climb, yet the most well known is from Bomerano. You can arrive at Bomerano by transport or vehicle from Positano. There is no extra charge for the climb, yet wearing agreeable shoes and bring a lot of water is significant.

Villa Rufolo is a stunning Positano villa. It is a museum that was built in the 12th century. The estate is known for its nurseries, which are terraced and offer shocking perspectives on the ocean. The estate is open from 9am to 7pm day to day and the extra charge is €7.50 for grown-ups.

The "Forte di Positano" is a medieval fortress perched atop a hill with a view of the town. It was used to protect Positano from pirates and was built in the 13th century. Despite the fact that the fortress is now defunct, you can still walk around it and take in the views. The fortress costs €3 to enter and is open daily from 9 a.m. to 6 p.m.

## The following restaurants are within close proximity to these historic sites

In close proximity to the Chiesa di Santa Maria Assunta e Cripta Medievale is Ristorante Il Cavatappi. It serves customary Italian food and has a delightful perspective on the ocean.

La Sponda can be found close to the Sentiero degli Dei. It serves fish dishes and has an enormous porch with perspectives on the shore.

Lo Scoglio is situated close to the Manor Rufolo. It serves new fish and pasta dishes and has a heartfelt setting on a bluff sitting above the ocean.

Il Pirata is close to the Forte di Positano. It serves pizza and pasta dishes and has an exuberant climate.

# CHAPTER EIGHT

## CUSINE

### Local Positano Cusines

**Spaghetti alla Positano**

Spaghetti tossed with local lemon slices, fresh basil, and tomatoes is a traditional dish.

**Frutti di mare**

This is a fish platter that normally incorporates an assortment of fish, shellfish, and calamari.

**Veal Sorrentina**

Veal is cooked in a tomato sauce with capers, olives, and anchovies in this dish.

**Ravioli al limone**

The ravioli in this dish are stuffed with ricotta cheese and lemon zest before being tossed in a lemon sauce.

**Torta caprese**

Almonds, flour, cocoa powder, sugar, and eggs go into this chocolate and almond cake.

Limoncello: This is a lemon alcohol that is made with lemons, sugar, and liquor.

## Pasta with broccoli

Olive oil, broccoli, and pasta are tossed together in this dish.

Margherita Pizza: This is an exemplary Neapolitan pizza that is made with tomatoes, mozzarella cheddar, and basil.

## Involtini

These are pastries that are rolled up and filled with meat, cheese, or vegetables, among other things.

## Cozze gratinate

These are mussels that are prepared in a pureed tomatoes with breadcrumbs and cheddar.

## Pesce spada alla griglia

This is barbecued swordfish that is normally presented with a lemon wedge.

Baked eggplant is topped with mozzarella and Parmesan cheeses, tomato sauce, and other toppings.

Focaccia: Olive oil, flour, water, and salt are used to make this flatbread. Tomatoes, onions, or olives are commonly used as toppings.

### Gelato

This is a delectable Italian frozen yogurt that is made with new milk, cream, and sugar.

### Cappuccino

This is an espresso drink that is made with coffee, steamed milk, and frothed milk.

### Spremuta

This is a new pressed juice that is normally made with oranges, lemons, or grapefruits.

These are only a couple of the numerous delectable neighborhood foods that you can appreciate in Positano. With such countless choices to choose from, you make certain to buy something as you would prefer.

# CHAPTER NINE

## TIPS AND ADVICE

### Advice for People Visiting Positano

Prepare yourself for a lot of stairs: Because Positano is built on a cliff, there will be a lot of steps and steep streets. Walking shoes that fit well are a necessity.

Bring light: It is best to pack light and avoid carrying heavy luggage due to the narrow streets and hilly terrain. Think about bringing a backpack or small suitcase that is easy to move around in.

Utilize public transport: Positano can get very blocked, particularly during top vacationer season. To see nearby towns and attractions like Amalfi and Capri, take the bus system or ferries.

Beach necessities: The stunning beaches of Positano are renowned. For a peaceful day by the sea, don't forget to bring swimwear, a beach towel, and sunscreen.

Embrace the neighborhood cooking: Try the fresh produce, delicious seafood, and traditional dishes like limoncello and spaghetti alle vongole (spaghetti with clams). Positano has various cafés and bistros to take special care of various preferences.

Search for neighborhood items: Handmade ceramics and Positano's vibrant fashion scene are its trademarks. Investigate the nearby shops and stores for remarkable style finds and keepsakes.

Regard the neighborhood culture: Positano is a very close local area with its own traditions and customs. Dress modestly when going to churches, be aware of local customs, and follow proper protocol.

## Traditions and Customs in Positano

Celebrations and festivities: Throughout the year, Positano hosts a number of festivals, one of which is the August 15 Feast of Santa Maria Assunta, which is a major event in the town. During these celebrations, anticipate lively processions, music, and fireworks.

Traditions of religion: There are a lot of churches and chapels all over Positano because of the town's religious history. A significant landmark is the iconic dome of the Church of Santa Maria Assunta.

Break time: In the same way as other Mediterranean towns, Positano notices a rest period during the evening. A lot of businesses and shops might close for a few hours, usually between 1:00 and 4:00 p.m.

## Outdoor activities in Positano

Positano offers the following outdoor activities

### Hiking

A popular hiking trail with stunning views of the Amalfi Coast is the Path of the Gods. It's a moderate hike, so bring plenty of water and comfortable

### Boating

There are various boat visits accessible in Positano, from basic roadtrips to additional courageous outings. You can go boating along the Amalfi Coast or even to Capri or Ischia.

### Swimming

Positano has some of the world's most stunning beaches. Absorb the sun, swim free waters, or take a boat out to the ocean.

### Paragliding

The Amalfi Coast can be seen from above thanks to paragliding. Positano has a lot of companies that offer paragliding tours.

### Cliff jumping

Cliff jumping is a popular Positano activity if you want an adrenaline rush. You can jump from the cliffs into the water at a number of locations along the coast.

### Stand-up paddleboarding

Stand-up paddleboarding is an extraordinary method for investigating the shoreline of Positano. You can paddle along the sea shores, or even venture out onto the ocean and investigate the caverns and channels.

These are just a few of Positano's many outdoor activities. You'll have a great time exploring this beautiful town and its surroundings, no matter which option you choose.

## Here is a possible Positano itinerary for 10 days

Day 1: Show up in Positano and look into your inn. Explore the town's colorful houses and winding streets for the afternoon. Dinner with a view of the sea can be enjoyed leisurely in the evening.

Day 2: Go on a boat outing to Capri and investigate the island's popular Blue Cavern. In the early evening, return to Positano and loosen up near the ocean.

Day 3: Take the difficult but rewarding hike known as the Path of the Gods, which offers breathtaking views of the Amalfi Coast.

Day 4: Visit the town of Ravello, which is roosted high over the Amalfi Coast and offers staggering perspectives on the shore. In the early evening, take a cooking class and figure out how to make customary Amalfi Coast dishes.

Day 5: Take a day trip to Amalfi. One if the towns in Amalfi coast

Day 6: Positano's beach is a great place to unwind and enjoy the sun. At night, partake in a heartfelt supper at one of the town's numerous cliffside cafés.

Day 7: Go on a boat outing to the island of Ischia, which is known for its warm showers. Enjoy the island's natural splendor while relaxing in the hot springs.

Day 8: spend a day at some of the historical places in Positano eg Villa Rufolo

Day 9: Go on a boat outing to the town of Minori, which is a more modest and more quiet town than Positano or Amalfi. Go through the day loosening up near the ocean or investigating the town's thin roads.

**Day 10:** Leave from Positano and head home.

You are free to alter this itinerary to suit your interests and time constraints because it is only a suggestion. Regardless of how you decide to invest your energy in Positano, you're certain to have a critical excursion.

The following are additional travel planning suggestions:

Spring and fall are the best times to visit Positano due to the mild weather and smaller crowds.

Assuming you're anticipating climbing the Way of the Divine beings, make certain to wear agreeable shoes and bring a lot of water.

Book your tickets in advance if you want to visit Herculaneum or Pompeii because they can sell out quickly.

Because Positano is a fairly pricey town, you can expect to pay a little more for food and lodging than you might in other parts of Italy.

Stunning views of the Amalfi Coast can be found from any location in Positano. So take as much time as is needed, unwind, and partake in the view.

Printed in Great Britain
by Amazon

45882972R00036